Content Page

Designed to reinforce essential math SKILLS!

By completing this math workbook, your child will gain systematic practice in the following math concepts:

- Counting by 1's, 2's, 5's and 10's
- Ordering Numbers
- Addition facts to 12
- Subtraction facts to 12
- Identifying Shapes
- Extending Patterns
- Drawing Shapes on a Grid
- Reading a Pictograph
- Beginning Fractions
- Beginning Measurement
- Telling Time

Content Development by Demetra Georgopoulos

Count and Write

a. Look at the picture. How many of each shape?

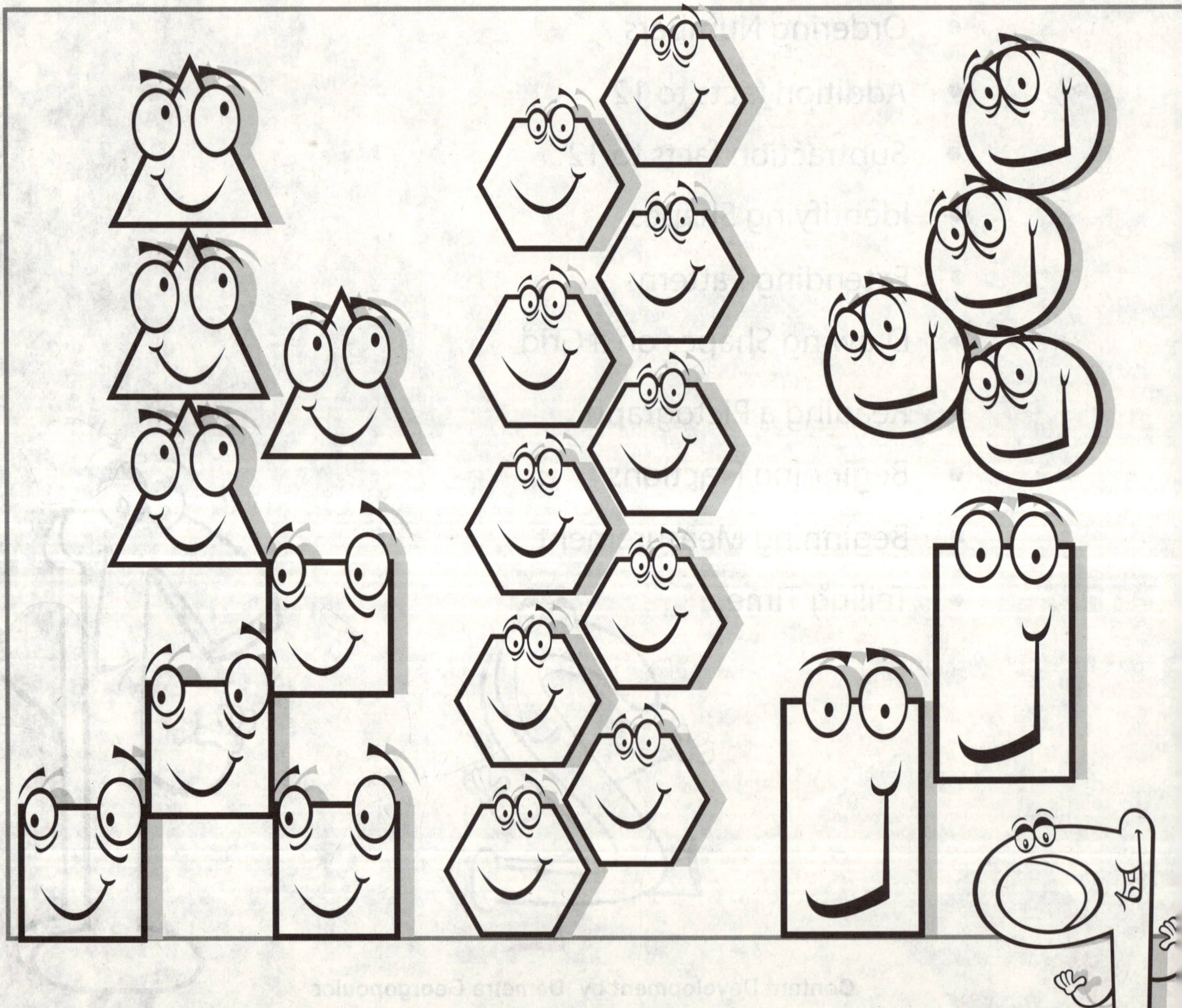

More and Less

a. Complete the following more or less sets.

Circle the set that has **less.**

1.

Circle the set that has **more.**

2.

Circle the set that has **less.**

3.

Circle the set that has **more.**

4.

Ordering Numbers

a. Order each group of numbers from **smallest** to **largest**.

Use the number line to help.

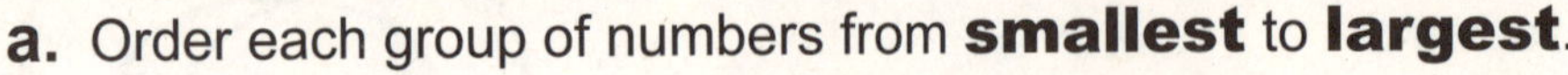

1. **7, 1, 8** ___1___, ___7___, ___8___
2. **2, 3, 4** ______, ______, ______
3. **9, 6, 5** ______, ______, ______
4. **0, 10, 3** ______, ______, ______
5. **7, 4, 8** ______, ______, ______
6. **6, 0, 1** ______, ______, ______
7. **10, 9, 5** ______, ______, ______
8. **5, 3, 2** ______, ______, ______
9. **10, 8, 0** ______, ______, ______
10. **9, 4, 1** ______, ______, ______
11. **7, 6, 2** ______, ______, ______
12. **4, 10, 3** ______, ______, ______

Number Maze 

a. Count by 1's. Help the big number 1 reach the big number 2.

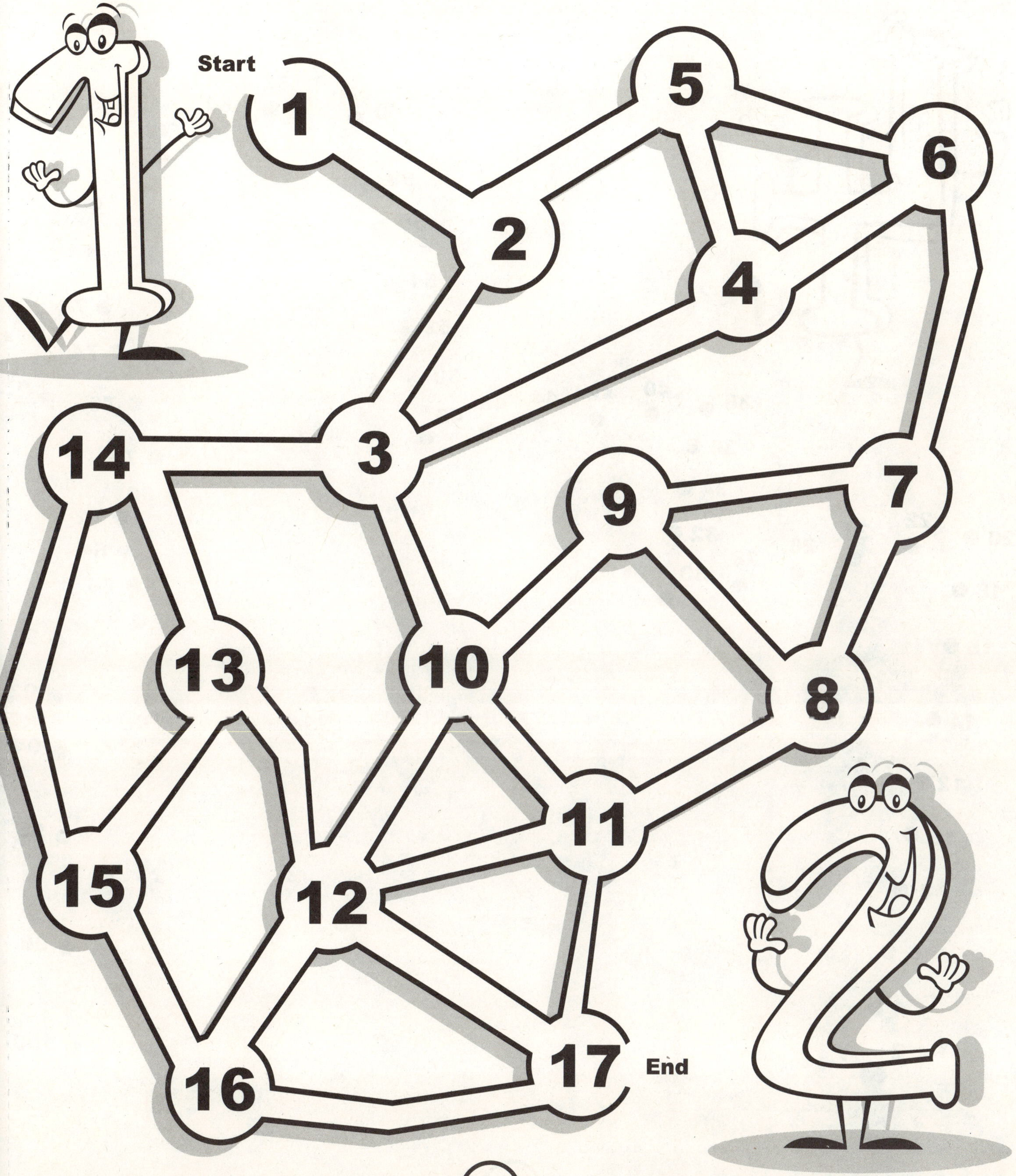

Start

1 2 3 4 5 6 7 8 9 10 11 12 13 14 15 16 17

End

Connect the Dots 

a. Connect the dots, counting by 2's to 100.

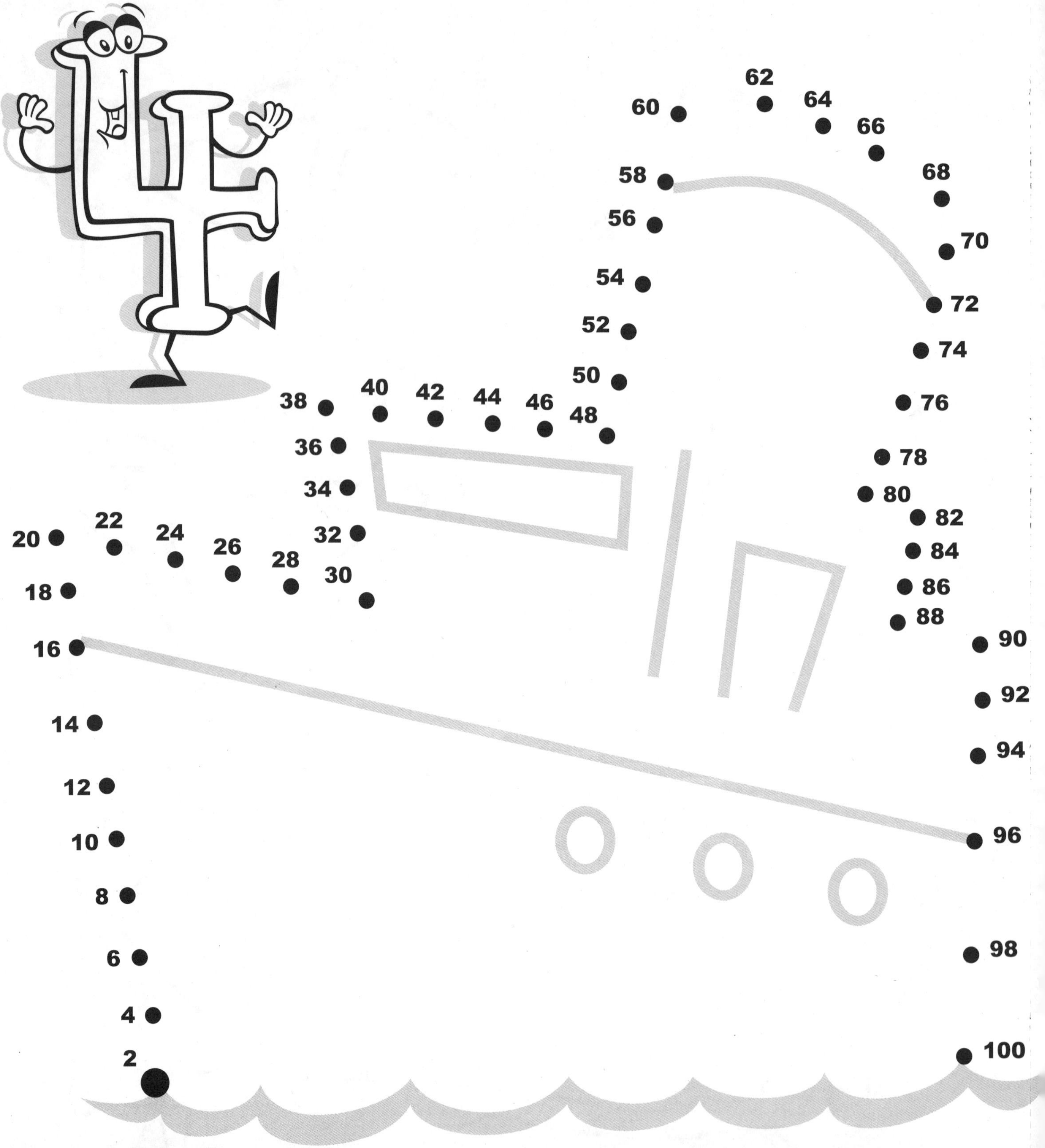

2 4 6 8 10 12 14 16 18 20 22 24 26 28 30 32 34 36 38 40 42 44 46 48 50 52 54 56 58 60 62 64 66 68 70 72 74 76 78 80 82 84 86 88 90 92 94 96 98 100

Connect the Dots 

a. Connect the dots, counting by 5's to 100.

5

100 10

95 15

90 20

85 25

30

80

75 35

40

70 55

60 50

65 45

Connect the Dots

a. Connect the dots, counting by 10's to 100.

Tens and Ones

a. Count and then write the tens and ones. Write how many blocks in all.

1.

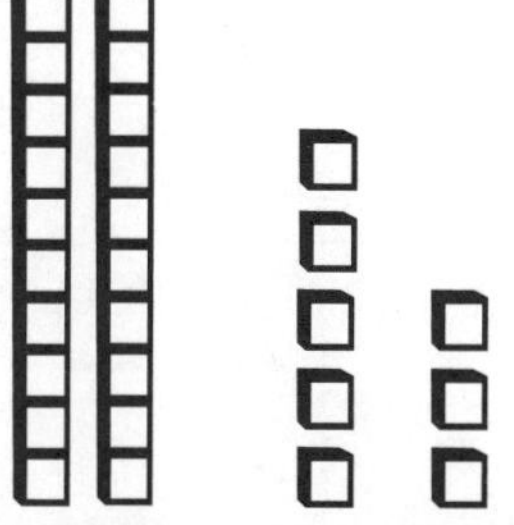

tens 20 ones 8

Write the number: 28

2.

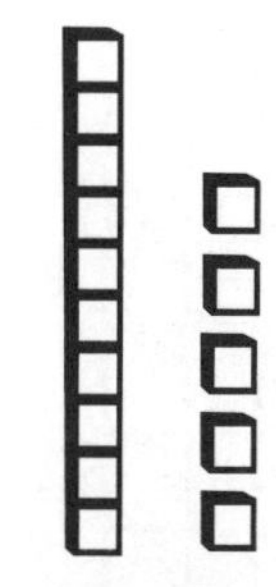

tens ☐ ones ☐

Write the number: ☐

3.

tens ☐ ones ☐

Write the number: ☐

4.

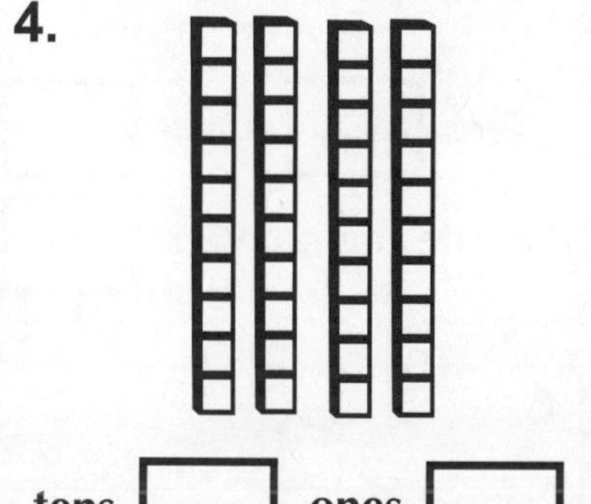

tens ☐ ones ☐

Write the number: ☐

5.

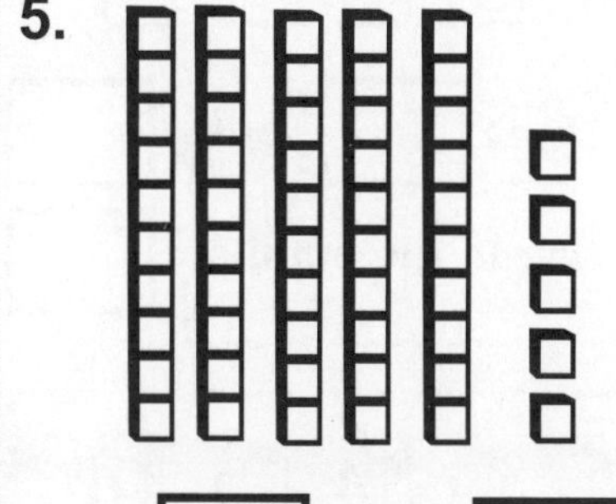

tens ☐ ones ☐

Write the number: ☐

6.

tens ☐ ones ☐

Write the number: ☐

7.

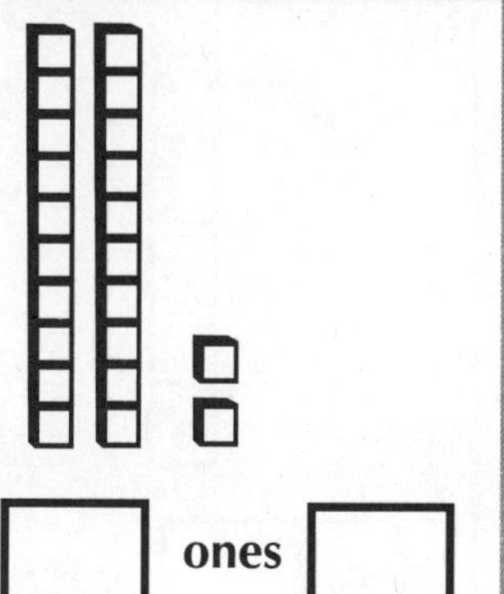

tens ☐ ones ☐

Write the number: ☐

8.

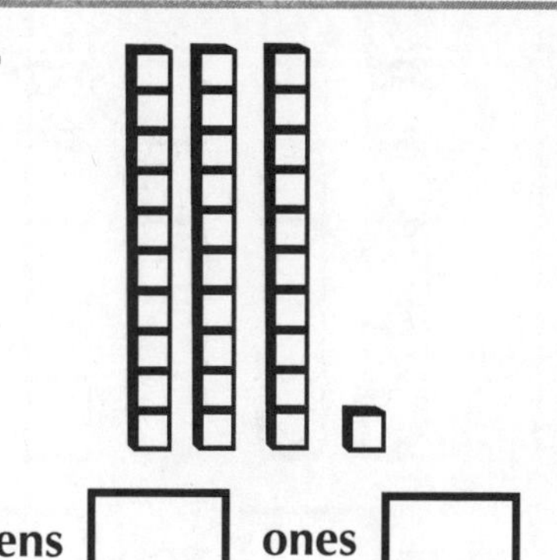

tens ☐ ones ☐

Write the number: ☐

9.

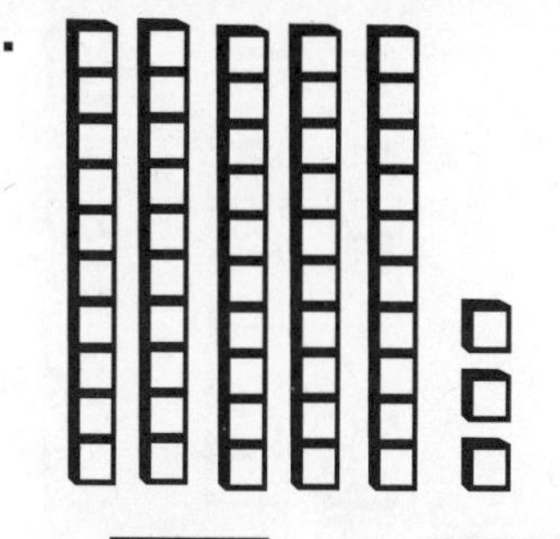

tens ☐ ones ☐

Write the number: ☐

Tens and Ones

a. Count and then write the tens and ones. Write how many blocks in all.

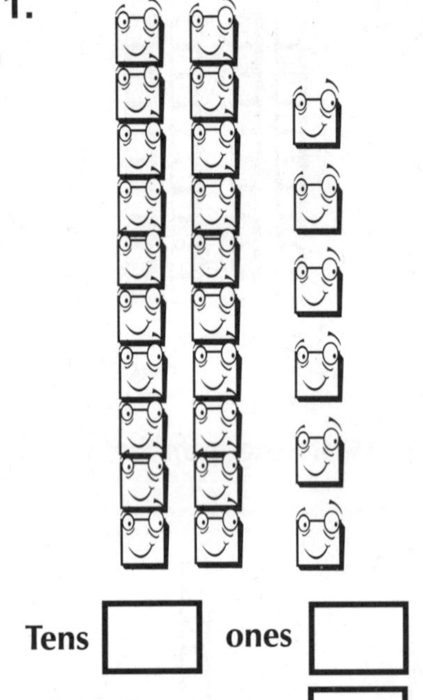

1.

Tens ☐ ones ☐

Write the number: ☐

2.

Tens ☐ ones ☐

Write the number: ☐

3.

Tens ☐ ones ☐

Write the number: ☐

4.

Tens ☐ ones ☐

Write the number: ☐

5.

Tens ☐ ones ☐

Write the number: ☐

6.

Tens ☐ ones ☐

Write the number: ☐

Addition Fun

a. Add the shapes together and complete the addition facts.

1.

______ + ______ = ______

2.

______ + ______ = ______

3.

______ + ______ = ______

4.

______ + ______ = ______

Addition Fun

a. Add the shapes together and complete the addition facts.

1.

_____ + _____ = _____

2.

_____ + _____ = _____

3.

_____ + _____ = _____

4.

_____ + _____ = _____

Addition Facts: Sums to 12

a. Complete the following sums.

Use the number line to help.

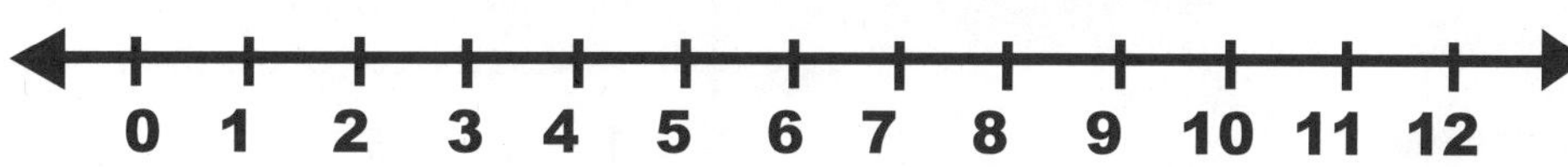

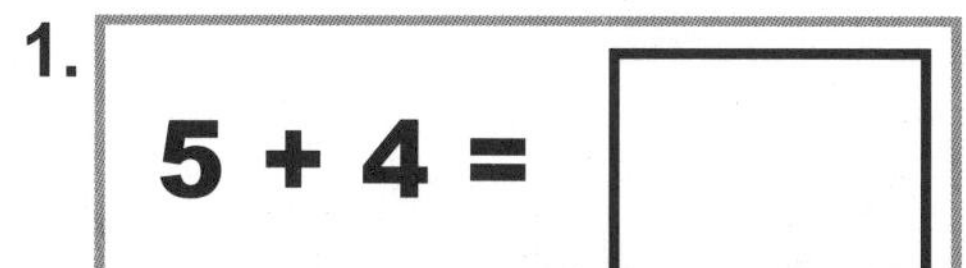

1. 5 + 4 = ☐
2. 2 + 6 = ☐
3. 4 + 2 = ☐
4. 2 + 2 = ☐
5. 8 + 4 = ☐
6. 3 + 3 = ☐
7. 4 + 4 = ☐
8. 4 + 3 = ☐
9. 2 + 3 = ☐
10. 7 + 5 = ☐
11. 1 + 5 = ☐
12. 2 + 7 = ☐
13. 5 + 5 = ☐
14. 7 + 2 = ☐
15. 4 + 7 = ☐
16. 3 + 2 = ☐
17. 6 + 5 = ☐
18. 3 + 9 = ☐

a. Complete the following sums.

Use the number line to help.

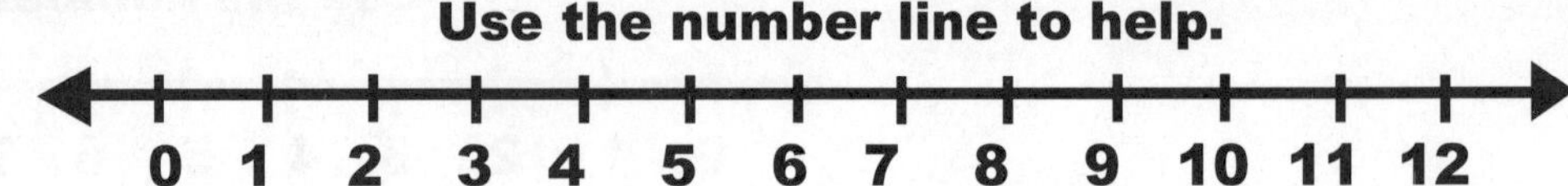

1. 2 + 2 = ☐
2. 3 + 1 = ☐
3. 5 + 5 = ☐
4. 7 + 2 = ☐
5. 8 + 3 = ☐
6. 2 + 4 = ☐
7. 1 + 3 = ☐
8. 6 + 2 = ☐
9. 2 + 8 = ☐
10. 4 + 2 = ☐
11. 2 + 5 = ☐
12. 5 + 3 = ☐
13. 6 + 6 = ☐
14. 2 + 1 = ☐
15. 5 + 4 = ☐
16. 3 + 9 = ☐

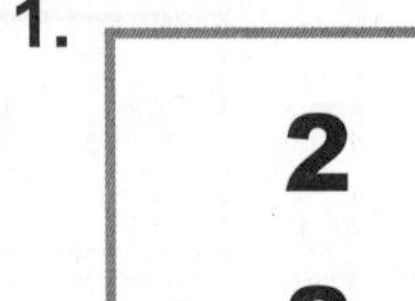
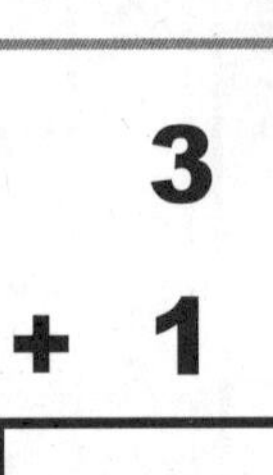
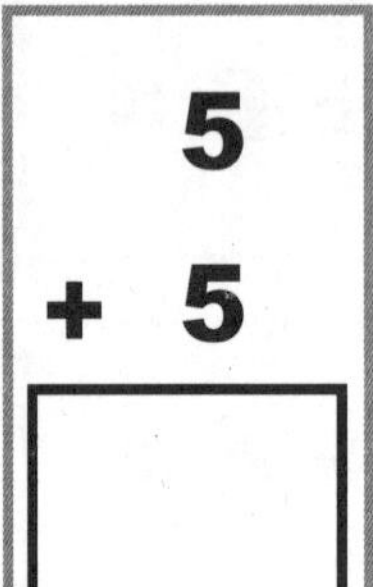
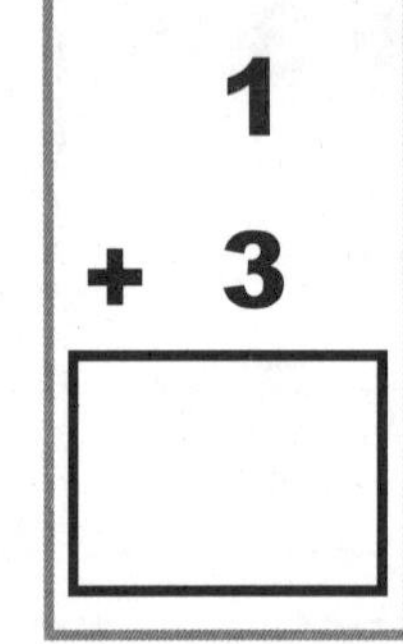
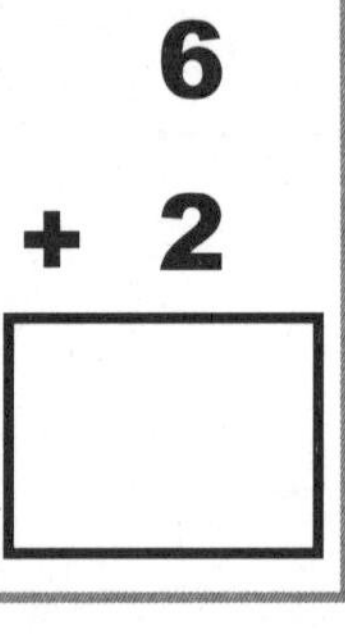

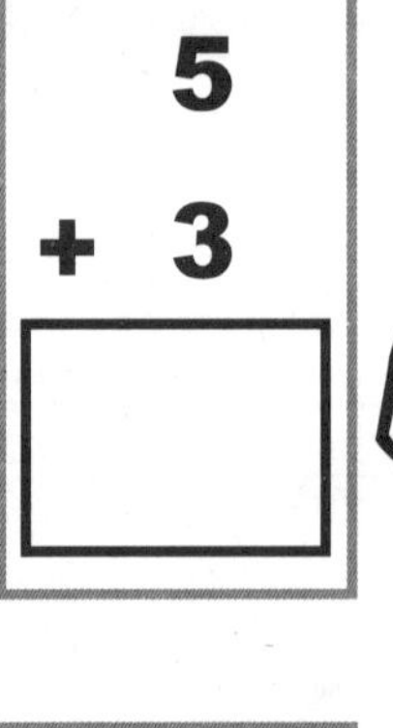
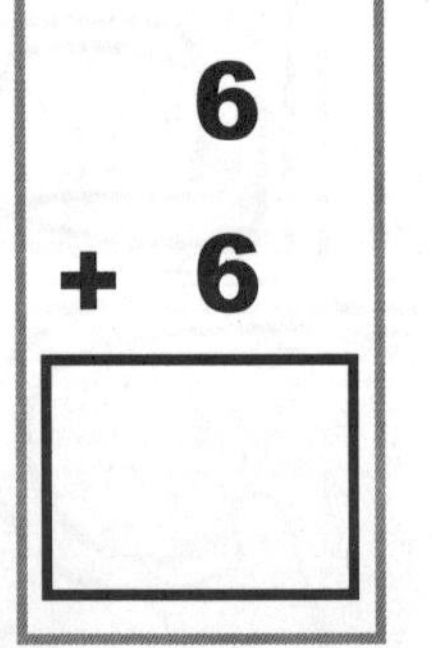

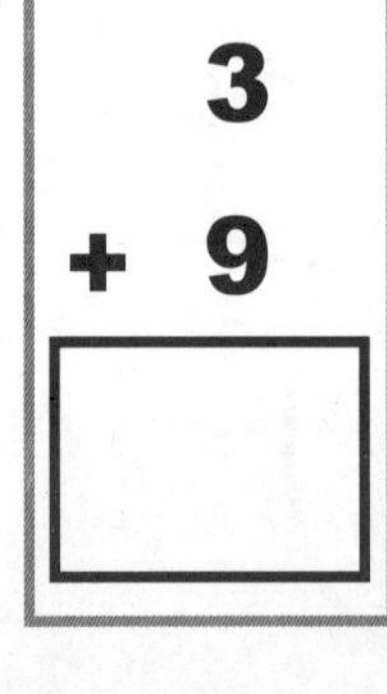

a. Complete the following sums.

1. ___ + ___ =

2. 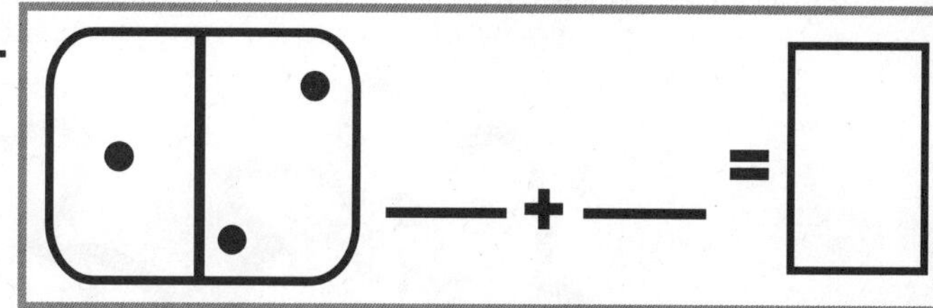
___ + ___ =

3. ___ + ___ =

4. 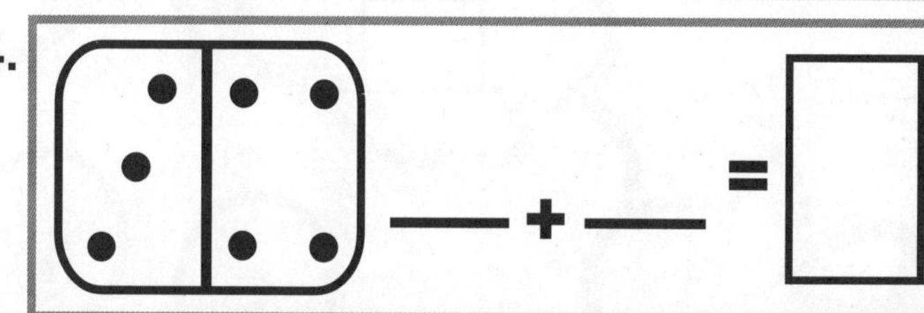
___ + ___ =

5. ___ + ___ =

6. 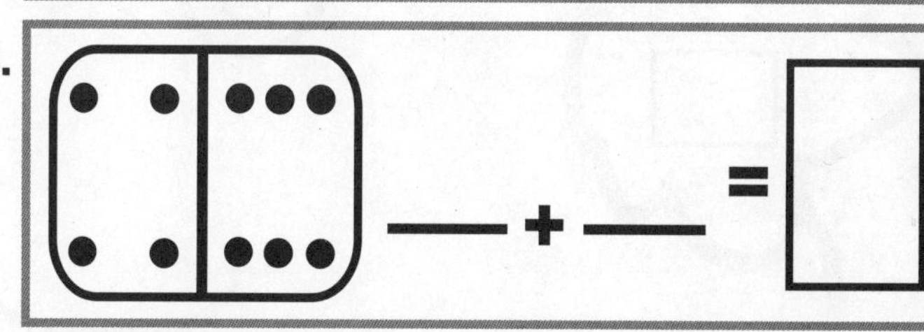
___ + ___ =

7. ___ + ___ =

8. 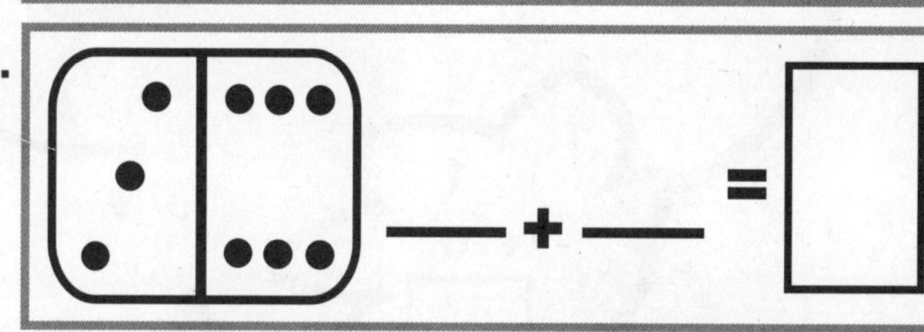
___ + ___ =

9. ___ + ___ =

10. 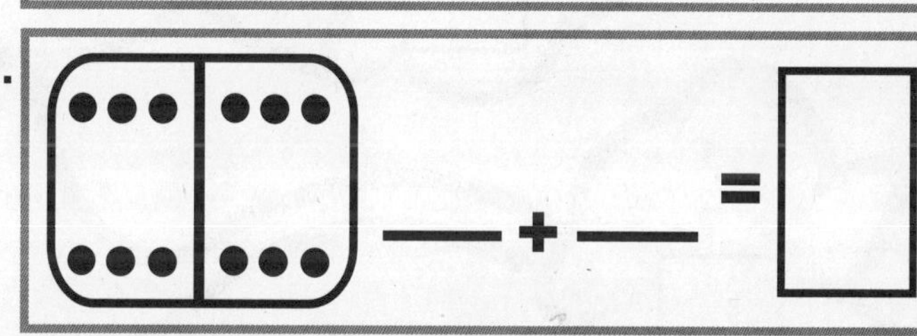
___ + ___ =

11. ___ + ___ =

12. 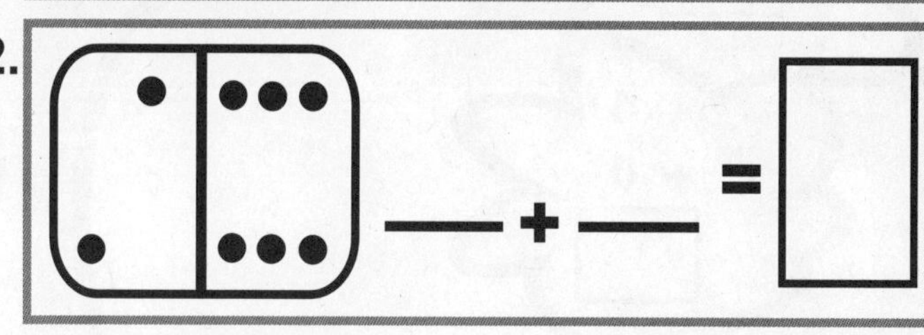
___ + ___ =

13. ___ + ___ =

14. 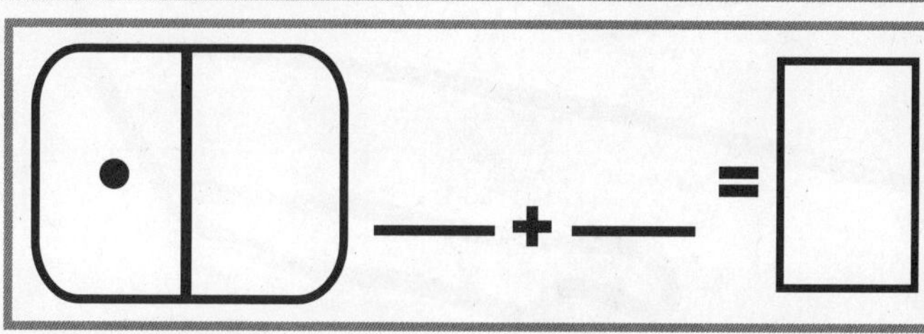
___ + ___ =

Addition Fun

Colour Key

If the answer is **1** colour **red.**
If the answer is **2** colour **blue.**
If the answer is **3** colour **green.**
If the answer is **4** colour **orange.**
If the answer is **5** colour **purple.**
If the answer is **6** colour **yellow.**

a. Complete the addition facts and use the colour key to colour the picture.

$0 + 1 = \square$

$2 + 0 = \square$

$2 + 2 = \square$

$3 + 0 = \square$

$1 + 2 = \square$

$3 + 1 = \square$

$1 + 0 = \square$

$2 + 4 = \square$

$1 + 1 = \square$

$5 + 0 = \square$

$4 + 0 = \square$

$3 + 2 = \square$

Sum Match

a. Match each sum to its answer.

1. **4 + 4 =**
2. **1 + 0 =**
3. **2 + 2 =**
4. **6 + 0 =**
5. **5 + 5 =**
6. **1 + 2 =**
7. **7 + 4 =**
8. **6 + 6 =**
9. **3 + 6 =**
10. **5 + 2 =**
11. **1 + 1 =**
12. **2 + 3 =**

12
8
6
5
9
2
4
10
1
3
7
11

Subtraction Practice

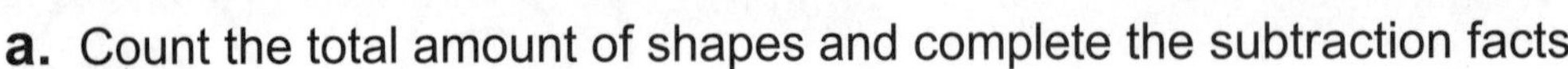

a. Count the total amount of shapes and complete the subtraction facts.

1.

_____ − _____ = _____

2.

_____ − _____ = _____

3.

_____ − _____ = _____

4.

_____ − _____ = _____

Subtraction Practice

a. Count the total amount of shapes and complete the subtraction facts.

1.

______ – ______ = ______

2.

______ – ______ = ______

3.

______ – ______ = ______

4.

______ – ______ = ______

Subtraction Facts to 12

a. Complete the following differences.

Use the number line to help.

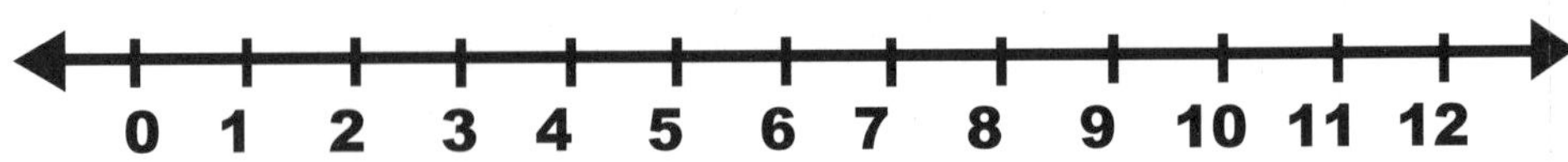

1. 10 - 6 = ☐
2. 12 - 6 = ☐
3. 1 - 0 = ☐
4. 4 - 2 = ☐
5. 6 - 2 = ☐
6. 8 - 2 = ☐
7. 10 - 7 = ☐
8. 8 - 3 = ☐
9. 5 - 3 = ☐
10. 9 - 8 = ☐
11. 9 - 5 = ☐
12. 3 - 1 = ☐
13. 11 - 5 = ☐
14. 12 - 4 = ☐
15. 8 - 4 = ☐
16. 7 - 4 = ☐
17. 6 - 1 = ☐
18. 9 - 3 = ☐

Subtraction Facts to 12

a. Complete the following differences.

Use the number line to help.

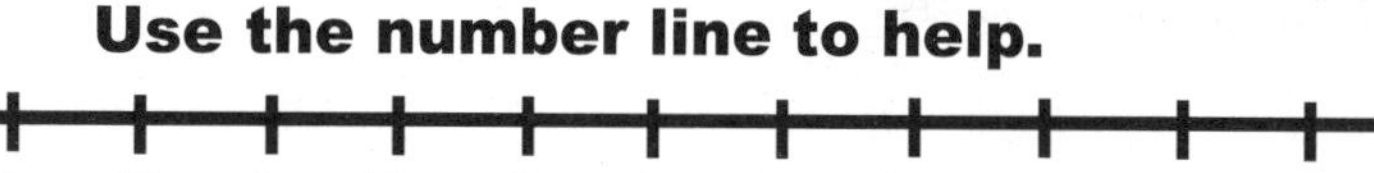

1. 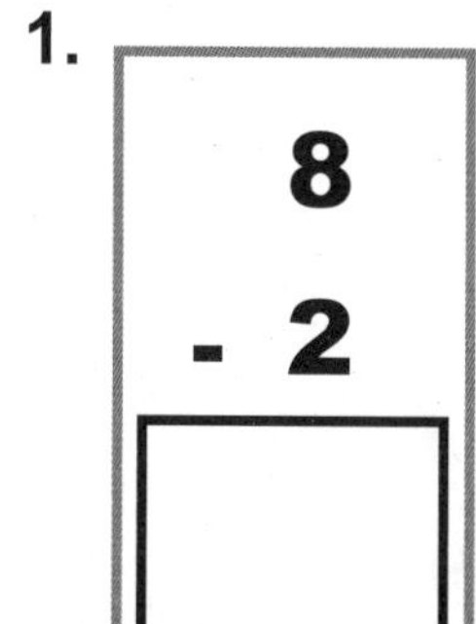
$8 - 2 = \square$

2. 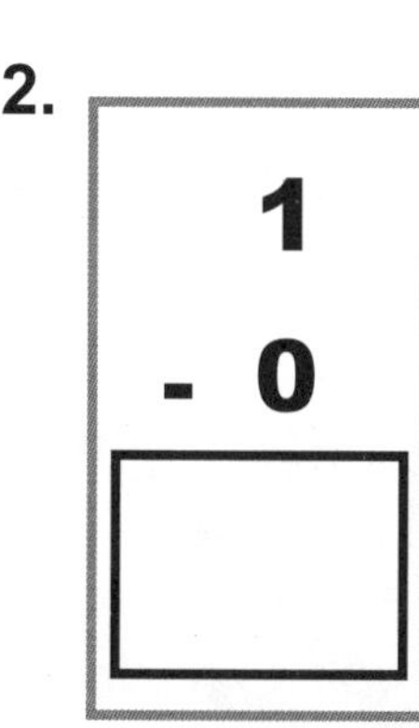
$1 - 0 = \square$

3. 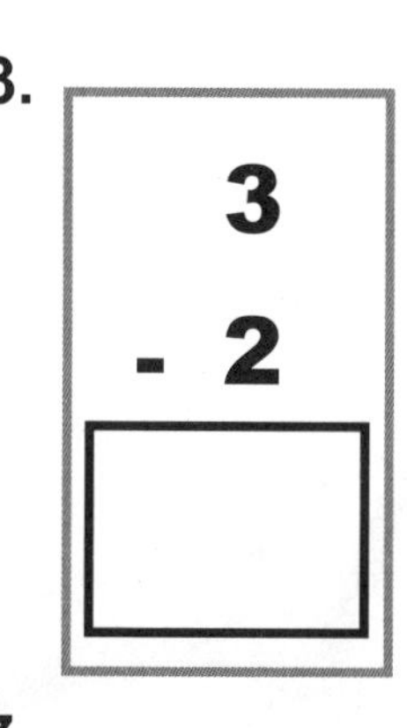
$3 - 2 = \square$

4. 
$10 - 4 = \square$

5. 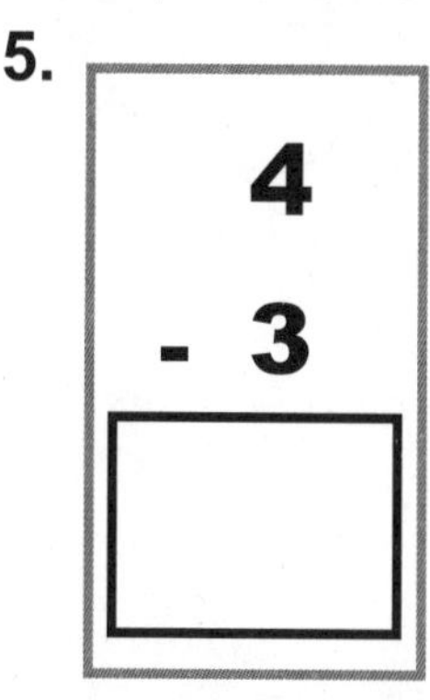
$4 - 3 = \square$

6. 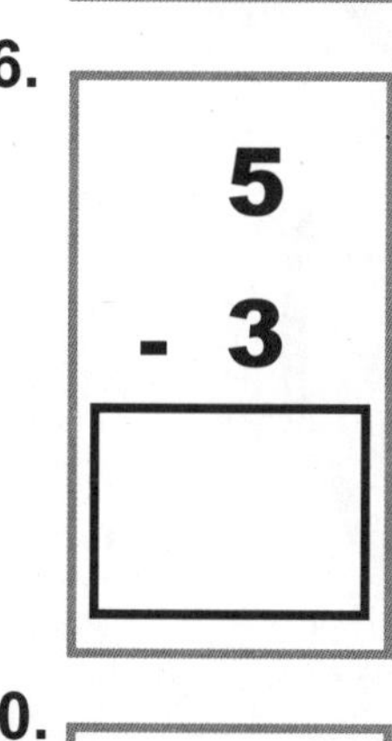
$5 - 3 = \square$

7. 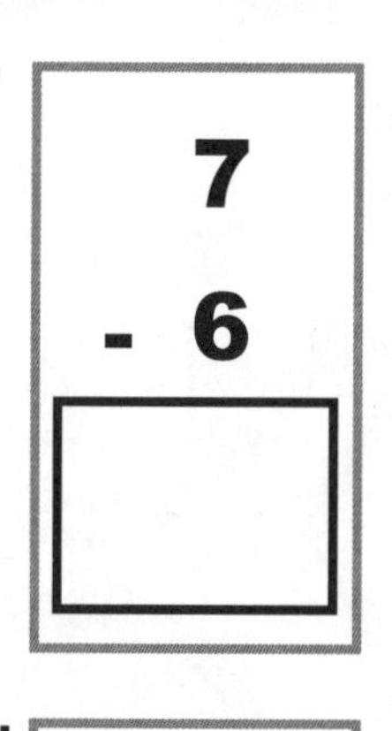
$7 - 6 = \square$

8. 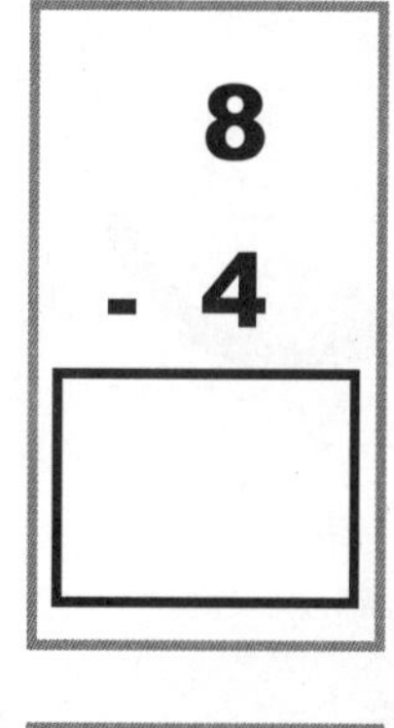
$8 - 4 = \square$

9. 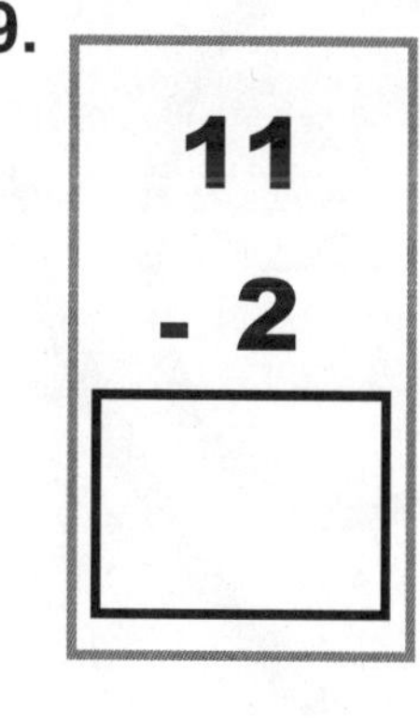
$11 - 2 = \square$

10. $8 - 6 = \square$

11. 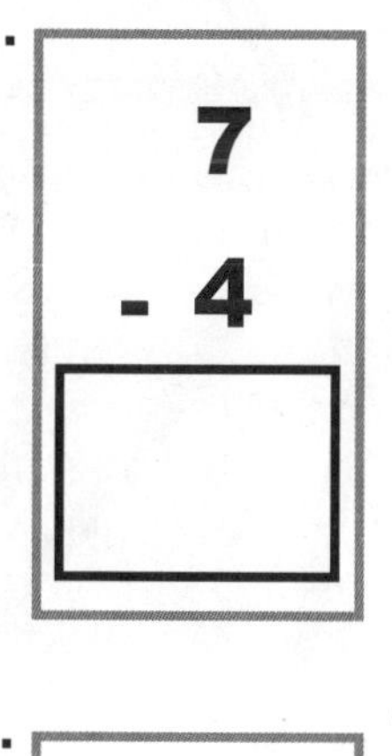
$7 - 4 = \square$

12. 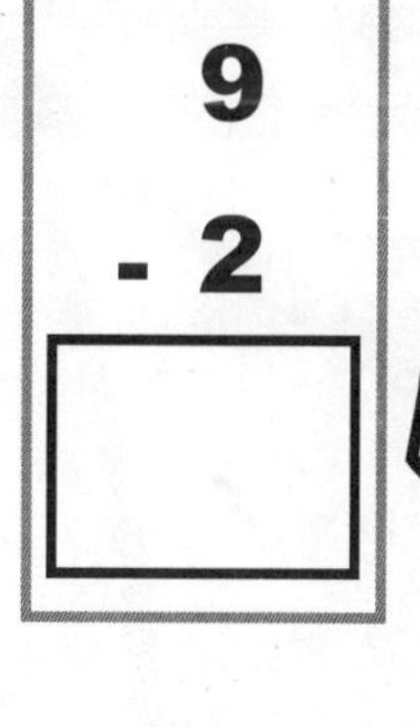
$9 - 2 = \square$

13. 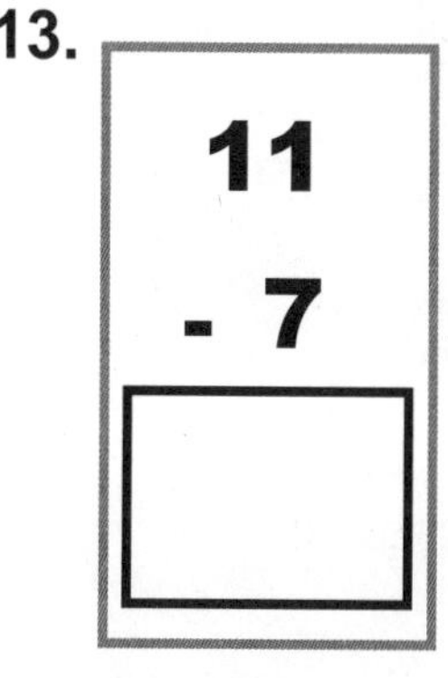
$11 - 7 = \square$

14. $10 - 5 = \square$

15. $7 - 5 = \square$

16. 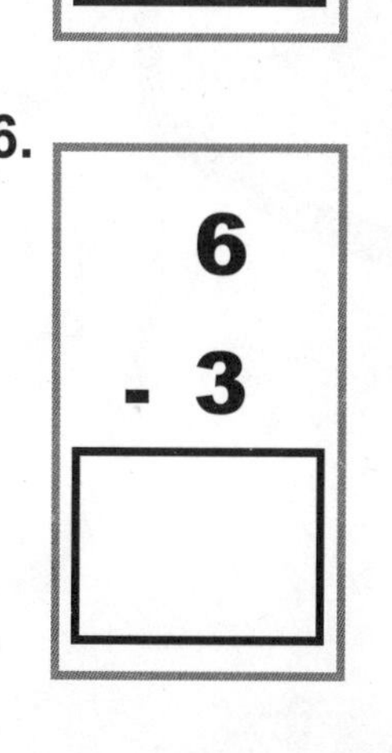
$6 - 3 = \square$

Subtraction Fun

Colour Key

If the answer is **1** colour **red.**
If the answer is **2** colour **blue.**
If the answer is **3** colour **green.**
If the answer is **4** colour **orange.**
If the answer is **5** colour **purple.**
If the answer is **6** colour **yellow.**

a. Complete the subtraction facts and use the colour key to colour the picture.

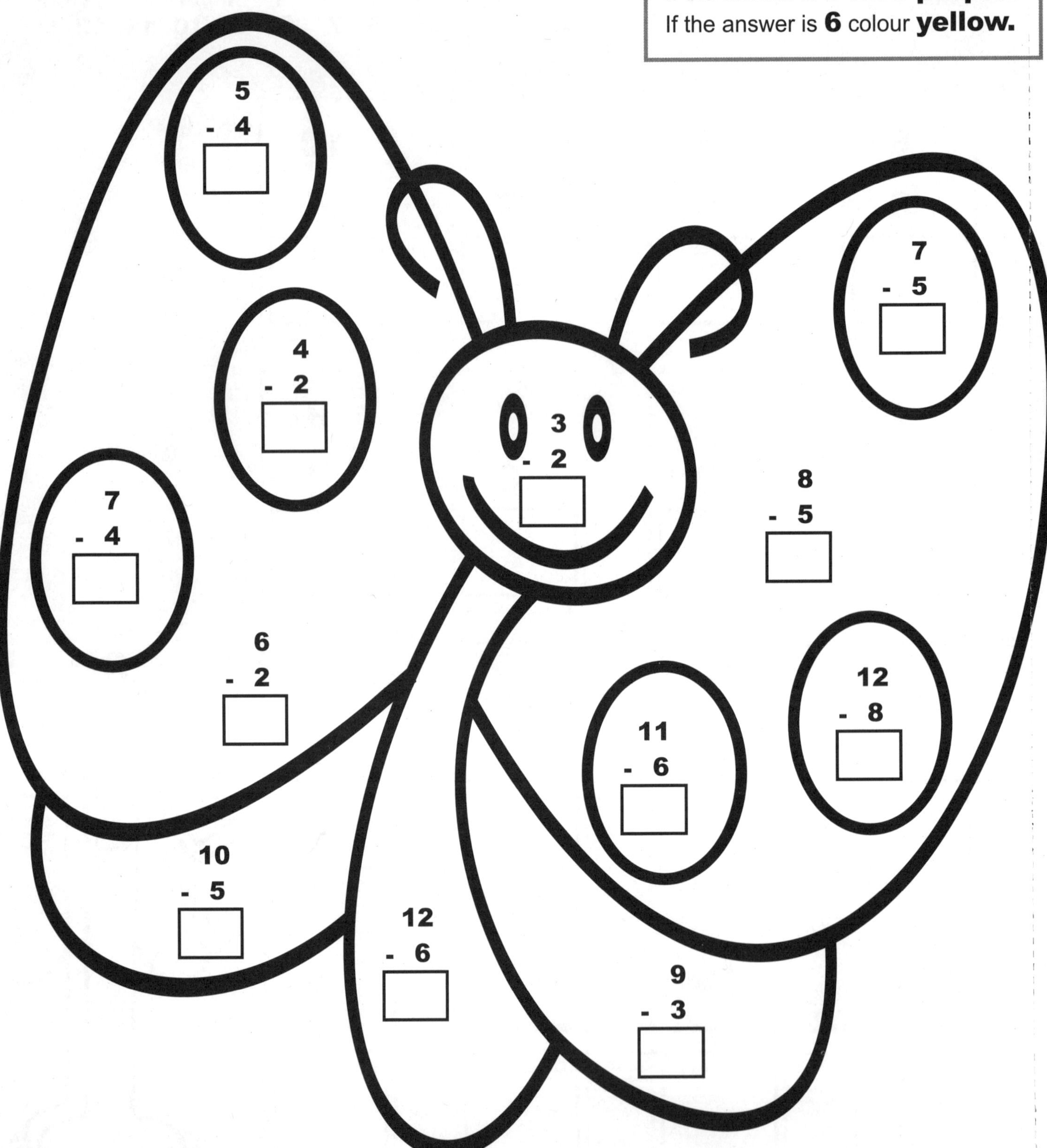

Subtraction Fun

a. Complete the subtraction facts and use the colour key to colour the picture.

Colour Key

If the answer is **1** colour **red.**
If the answer is **2** colour **blue.**
If the answer is **3** colour **green.**
If the answer is **4** colour **orange.**
If the answer is **5** colour **purple.**
If the answer is **6** colour **yellow.**

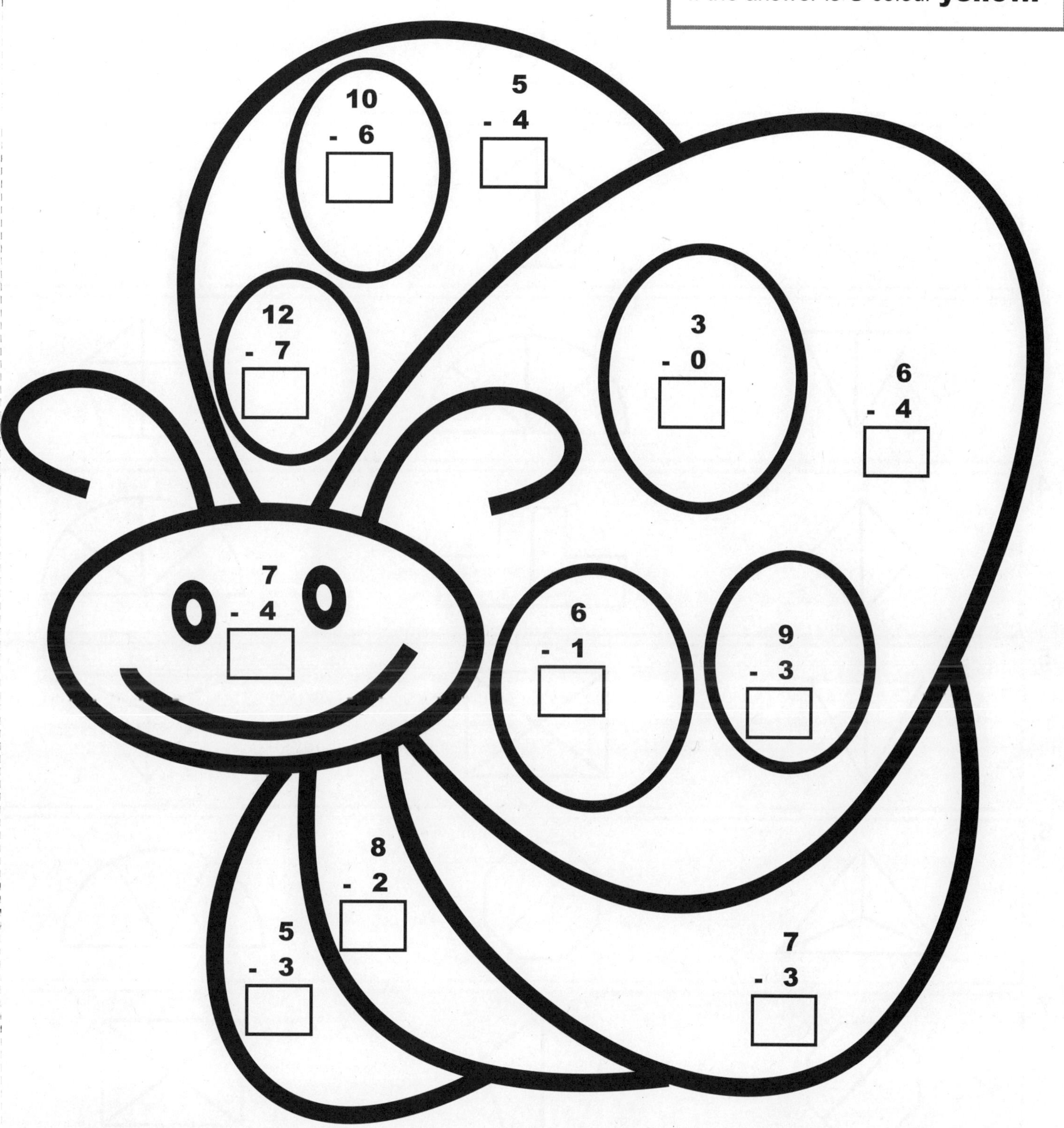

Halves

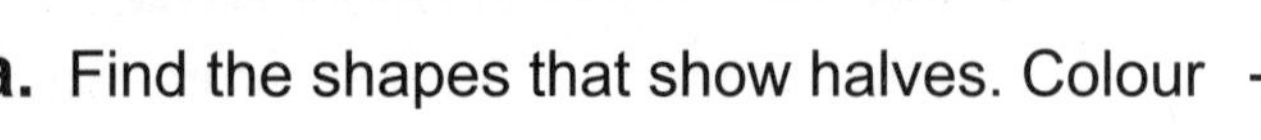

a. Find the shapes that show halves. Colour $\frac{1}{2}$

1. 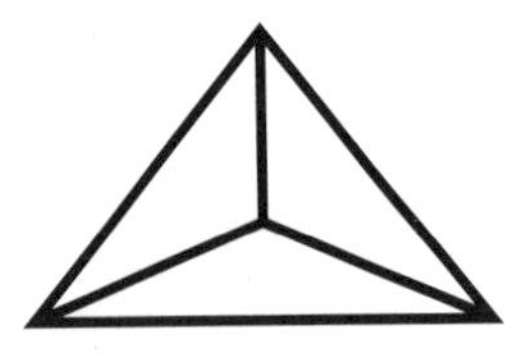 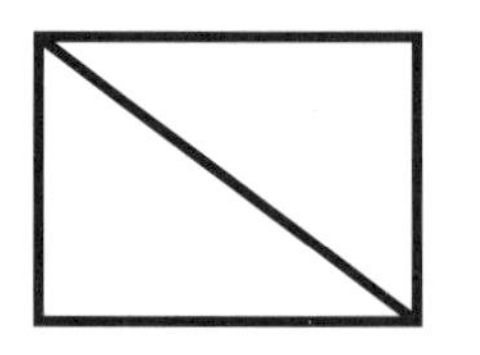

2. 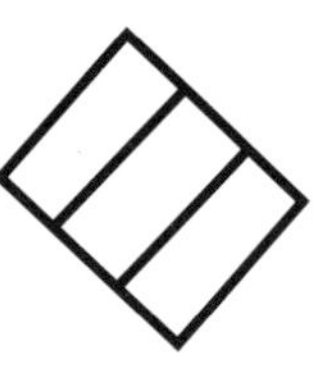 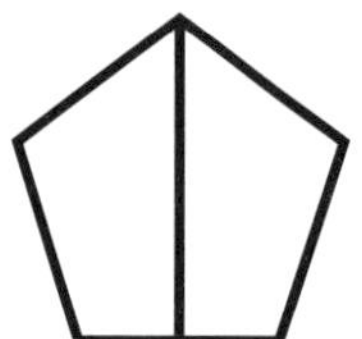 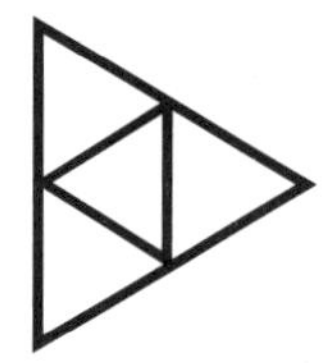

3. 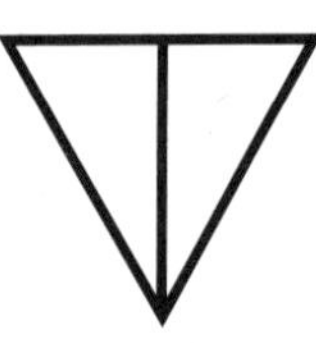 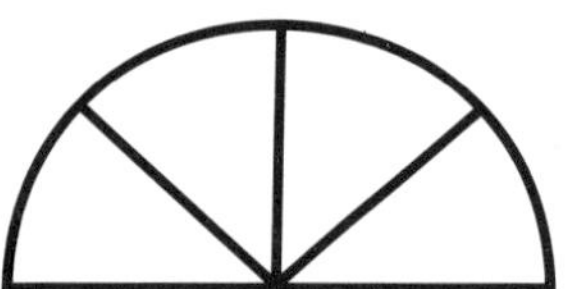 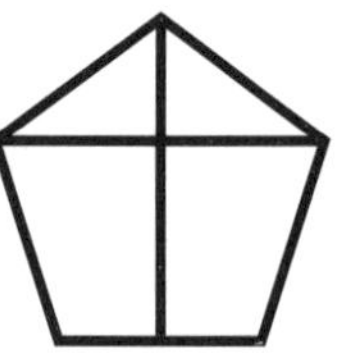

4. 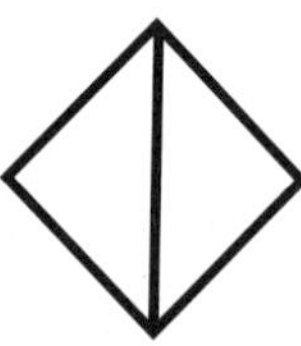 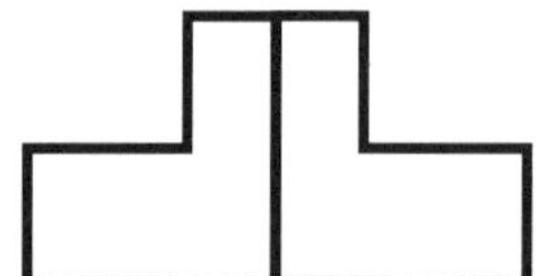 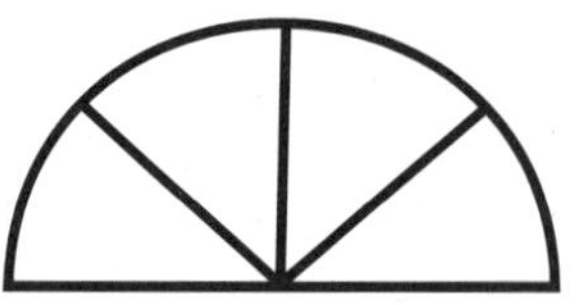

5. 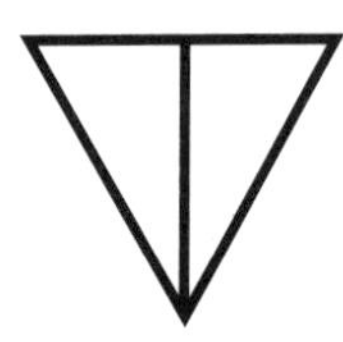  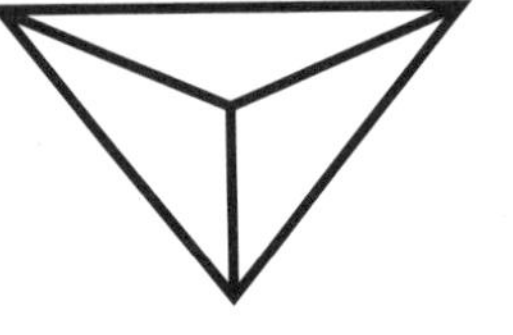

6. 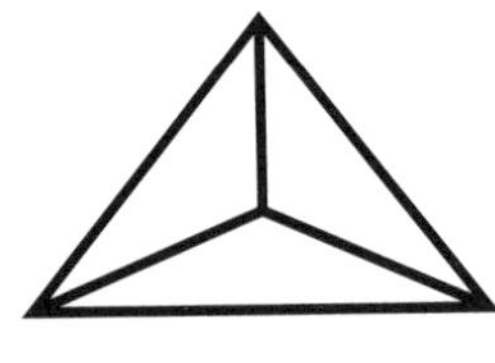  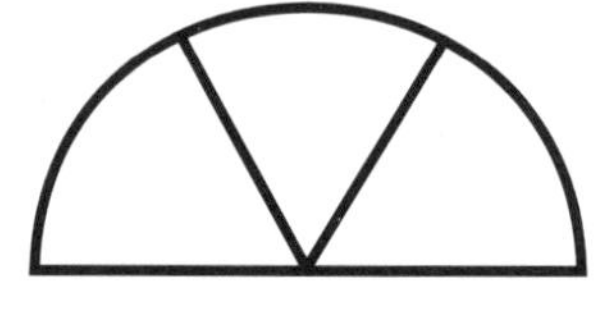

7.  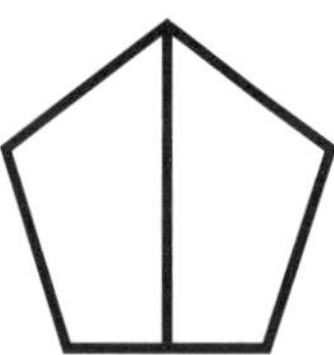 

Circle the Fractions

a. What fraction does the coloured part show? Circle the fraction.

1.

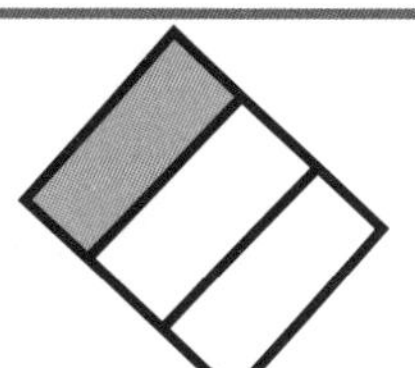

$\frac{1}{2}$ $\frac{1}{3}$ $\frac{1}{4}$

2.

$\frac{1}{2}$ $\frac{1}{3}$ $\frac{1}{4}$

3.

$\frac{1}{2}$ $\frac{1}{3}$ $\frac{1}{4}$

4.

$\frac{1}{2}$ $\frac{1}{3}$ $\frac{1}{4}$

5.

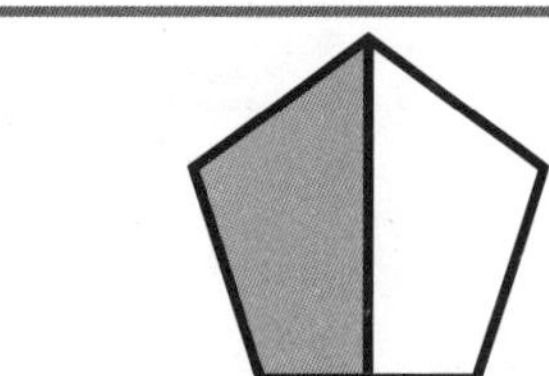

$\frac{1}{2}$ $\frac{1}{3}$ $\frac{1}{4}$

6.

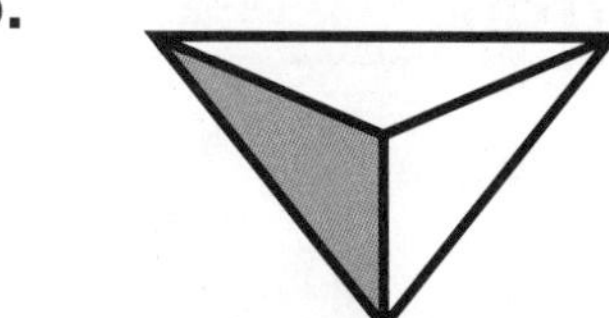

$\frac{1}{2}$ $\frac{1}{3}$ $\frac{1}{4}$

7.

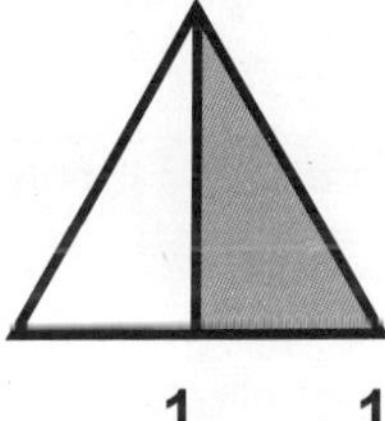

$\frac{1}{2}$ $\frac{1}{3}$ $\frac{1}{4}$

8.

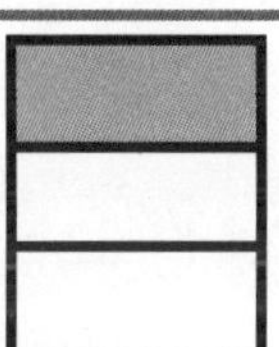

$\frac{1}{2}$ $\frac{1}{3}$ $\frac{1}{4}$

9.

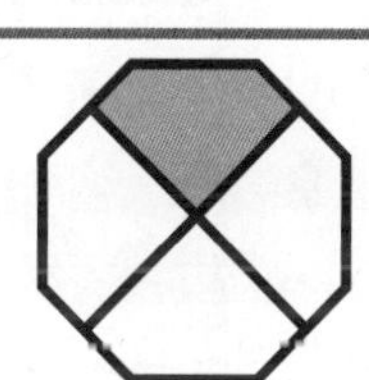

$\frac{1}{2}$ $\frac{1}{3}$ $\frac{1}{4}$

10.

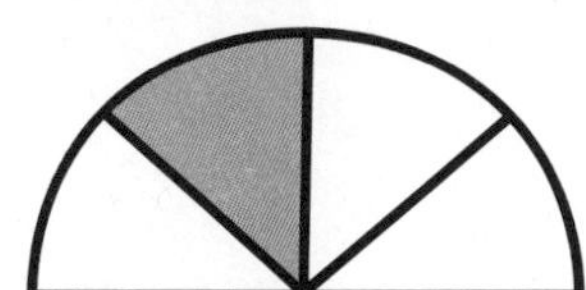

$\frac{1}{2}$ $\frac{1}{3}$ $\frac{1}{4}$

11.

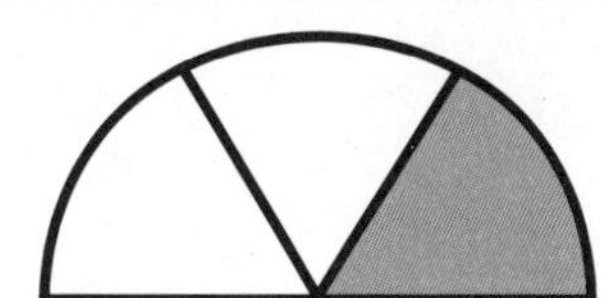

$\frac{1}{2}$ $\frac{1}{3}$ $\frac{1}{4}$

12.

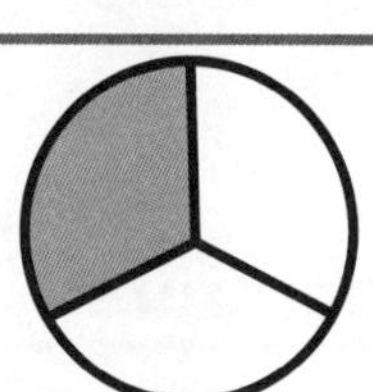

$\frac{1}{2}$ $\frac{1}{3}$ $\frac{1}{4}$

Drawing Shapes

a. Connect the dots to draw the shape and then draw your own without help.

		Connect The Dots	Draw Your Own
1.	rectangle		
2.	circle		
3.	triangle		
4.	square		
5.	rhombus		
6.	pentagon		

Get to Know Your Shapes!

a. How many sides and angles does each shape have?

		Number Of Sides	Number Of Angles
1.	rectangle		
2.	circle		
3.	triangle		
4.	square		
5.	rhombus		
6.	pentagon		

Read and Follow the Directions

a. Follow the directions and help the circle reach the triangle.

1. Start at the circle.

2. Move **right** 3 spaces.
3. Move **down** 3 spaces.
4. Move **left** 3 spaces.
5. Move **up** 2 spaces.
6. Move **right** 6 spaces.
7. Move **down** 3 spaces.

Draw Shapes on the Grid

a. Draw the shapes on the grid. The first one has been done for you.

A.

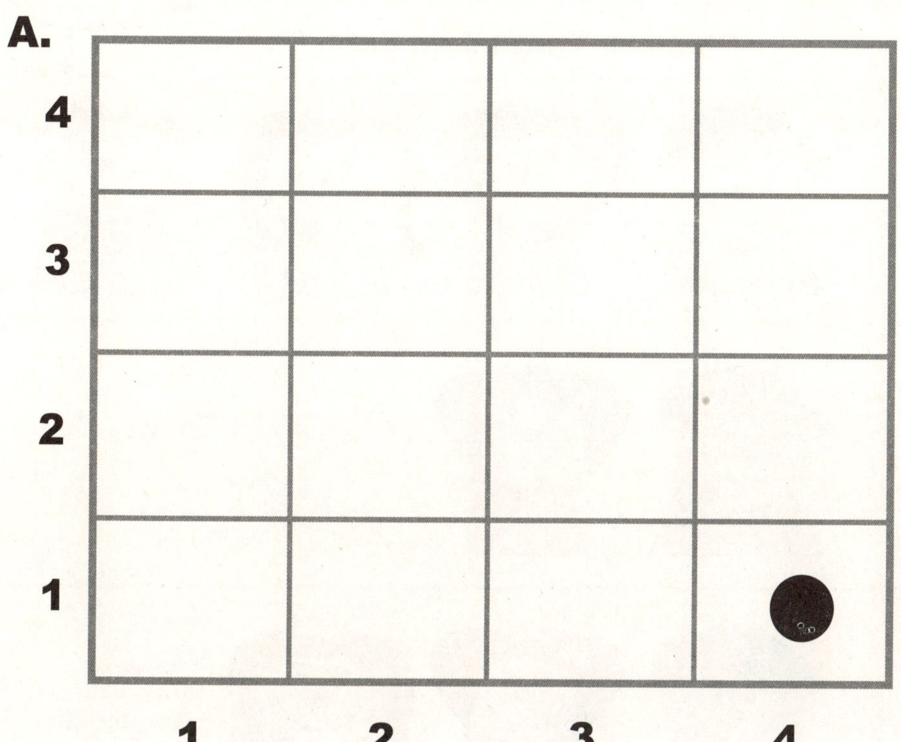

Draw ● at **(4 , 1)**

Draw ⬟ at **(3 , 4)**

Draw ■ at **(2 , 2)**

Draw ▲ at **(3 , 1)**

B.

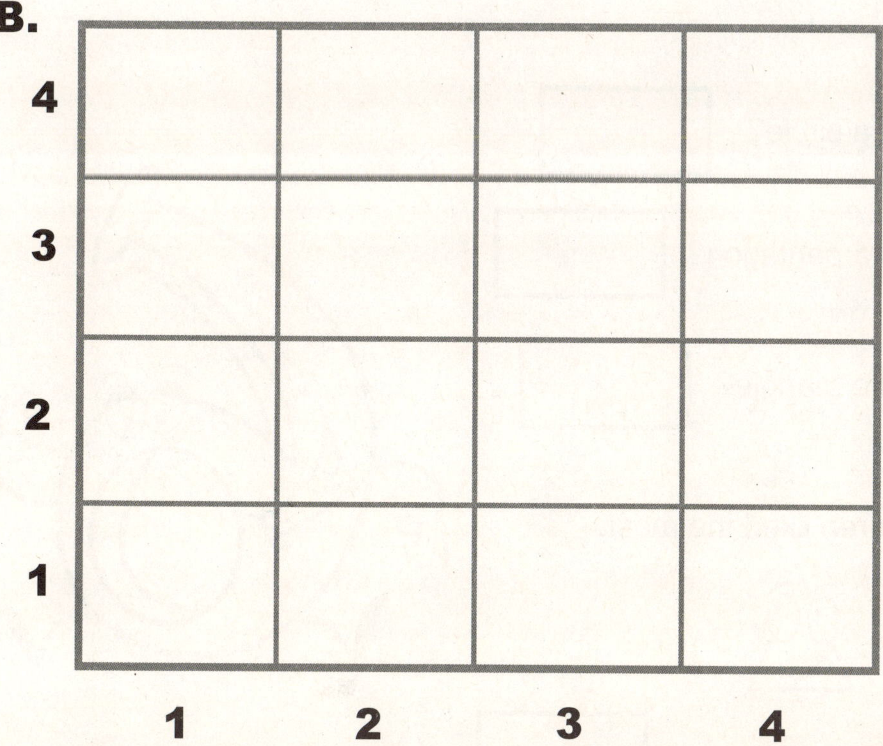

Draw ● at **(1 , 1)**

Draw ■ at **(2 , 3)**

Draw ⬟ at **(4 , 2)**

Draw ▲ at **(1 , 2)**

Shapes Pictograph 

a. Look at the shapes pictograph and answer the questions.

Kind Of Shape	Children That Liked Each Shape

1. How many children liked a circle? 

2. How many children liked a pentagon? 

3. How many children liked a triangle? 

4. Circle the shape the children liked the most.

5. How many children voted altogether? 

Measurment: How Long?

a. How long is each object?

1.

2.

3.

Tallest to Shortest

a. Number the pictures in each row from the **tallest** to the **shortest**.

1.

2.

Temperature: Hot and Cold

a. Is the temperature **hot** or **cold** in the picture? Circle the answer.

b. Draw your own picture.

Extending Patterns

a. Finish each pattern.

1. x] x] x] x]
2. * x * x * x
3. *] *] *]
4. x o x o x o
5.] *] *] *
6. o] o] o]

Telling Time 

a. Fill in the clock face with numbers to represent time.

12

Telling Time to the Hour

a. Write the time.

1.

_______ o' clock

2.

_______ o' clock

3.

_______ o' clock

4.

_______ o' clock

5.

_______ o' clock

6.

_______ o' clock

7.

_______ o' clock

8.

_______ o' clock

9.

_______ o' clock

10.

_______ o' clock

11.

_______ o' clock

12.

_______ o' clock

Telling Time to the Half Hour

a. Write the time.

1.

half past ______

2.
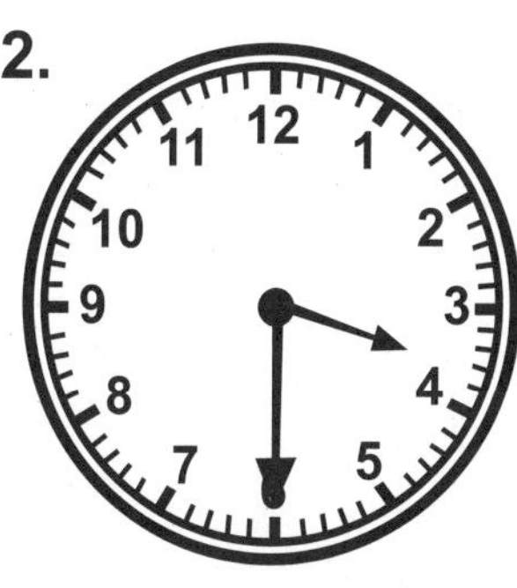
half past ______

3.

half past ______

4.

half past ______

5.

half past ______

6.

half past ______

7.

half past ______

8.

half past ______

9.

half past ______

10.

half past ______

11.

half past ______

12.

half past ______

Answer Page

Here are some answer pages from math book grade one.

Page **2** Count and Write

pentagon 10, circle 4, square 4, triangle 4, rectangle 2

Page **3** More or Less

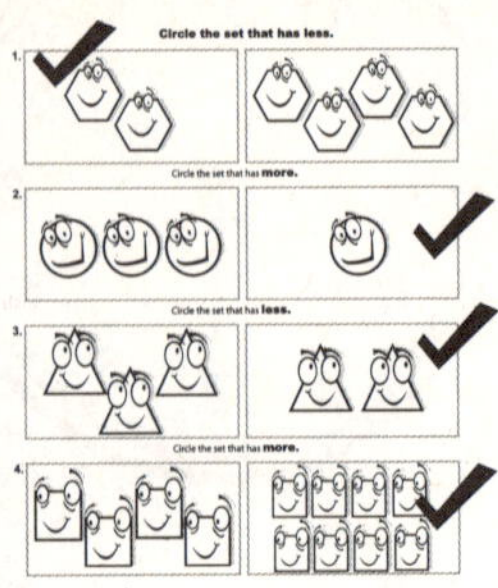

Page **4** Ordering Numbers

(1) 1, 7, 8 (2) 2, 3, 4 (3) 5, 6, 9 (4) 0, 3, 10 (5) 4, 7, 8 (6) 0, 1, 6 (7) 5, 9, 10 (8) 2, 3, 5 (9) 0, 8, 10 (10) 1, 4, 9
(11) 2, 6, 7 (12) 3, 4, 10

Page **9** Tens and Ones

(1) 2 tens, 8 ones = 28 (2) 1 tens, 5 ones = 15 (3) 4 tens, 4 ones = 44 (4) 4 tens, 0 ones = 40
(5) 5 tens, 5 ones = 55 (6) 1 tens, 2 ones = 12 (7) 2 tens, 2 ones = 22 (8) 3 tens, 1 ones = 31
(9) 5 tens, 3 ones = 53

Page **10** Tens and Ones

(1) 2 tens, 6 ones = 26 (2) 3 tens, 1 ones = 31 (3) 1 tens, 5 ones = 15 (4) 2 tens, 4 ones = 24
(5) 4 tens, 0 ones = 40 (6) 1 tens, 1 ones = 11

Page **11** Addition Fun

(1) 2 + 5 = 7 (2) 3 + 4 = 7 (3) 2 + 3 = 5 (4) 4 + 1 = 5

Page **12** Addition Fun

(1) 2 + 4 = 6 (2) 4 + 4 = 8 (3) 3 + 1 = 4 (4) 2 + 6 = 8

Page **13** Addition Facts: Sums to 12

(1) 9 (2) 8 (3) 6 (4) 4 (5) 12 (6) 6 (7) 8 (8) 7 (9) 5 (10) 12 (11) 6 (12) 9
(13) 10 (14) 9 (15) 11 (16) 5 (17) 11 (18) 12

Answer Page

Here are some answer pages from math book grade one.

Page **14** Addition Facts: Sums to 12

(1) 4 (2) 4 (3) 10 (4) 9 (5) 11 (6) 6 (7) 4 (8) 8 (9) 10 (10) 6 (11) 7 (12) 8
(13) 12 (14) 3 (15) 9 (16) 12

Page **15** Addition Facts: Sums to 12

(1) 1 + 4 = 5 (2) 1 + 2 = 3 (3) 3 + 0 = 3 (4) 3 + 4 = 7

(5) 4 + 4 = 8 (6) 4 + 6 = 10 (7) 5 + 6 = 11 (8) 3 + 6 = 9

(9) 1 + 6 = 7 (10) 6 + 6 = 12 (11) 2 + 0 = 2 (12) 2 + 6 = 8

(13) 2 + 5 = 7 (14) 1 + 0 = 1

Page **16** Addition Fun

(1) 0 + 1 = 1 (2) 2 + 0 = 2 (3) 3 + 0 = 3 (4) 1 + 2 = 3

(5) 3 + 1 = 4 (6) 2 + 4 = 6 (7) 5 + 0 = 5 (8) 3 + 2 = 5

(9) 4 + 0 = 4 (10) 1 + 1 = 2 (11) 1 + 0 = 1 (12) 2 + 2 = 4

Page **17** Sum Match

(1) 8 (2) 1 (3) 4 (4) 6 (5) 10 (6) 3 (7) 11 (8) 12 (9) 9 (10) 7 (11) 2 (12) 5

Page **18** Subtraction Practice

(1) 10 - 6 = 4 (2) 10 - 5 = 5 (3) 9 - 4 = 5 (4) 4 - 3 = 1

Page **19** Subtraction Practice

(1) 6 - 3 = 3 (2) 10 - 4 = 6 (3) 12 - 5 = 7 (4) 6 - 1 = 5

Page **20** Subtraction Facts: Facts to 12

(1) 4 (2) 6 (3) 1 (4) 2 (5) 4 (6) 6 (7) 3 (8) 5 (9) 2 (10) 1 (11) 4 (12) 2
(13) 6 (14) 8 (15) 4 (16) 3 (17) 5 (18) 6

Answer Page

Here are some answer pages from math book grade one.

Page **21** Subtraction Facts: Facts to 12

(1) 6 (2) 1 (3) 1 (4) 6 (5) 1 (6) 2 (7) 1 (8) 4 (9) 9 (10) 2 (11) 3 (12) 7
(13) 4 (14) 5 (15) 2 (16) 3

Page **22** Subtraction Fun

(1) 5 - 4 = 1 (2) 4 - 2 = 2 (3) 3 - 2 = 1 (4) 7 - 5 = 2

(5) 8 - 5 = 3 (6) 12 - 8 = 4 (7) 11 - 6 = 5 (8) 9 - 3 = 6

(9) 12 - 6 = 6 (10) 10 - 5 = 5 (11) 6 - 2 = 4 (12) 7 - 4 = 3

Page **23** Subtraction Fun

(1) 10 - 6 = 4 (2) 5 - 4 = 1 (3) 3 - 0 = 3 (4) 6 - 4 = 2

(5) 9 - 3 = 6 (6) 7 - 3 = 4 (7) 6 - 1 = 5 (8) 8 - 2 = 6

(9) 5 - 3 = 2 (10) 7 - 4 = 3 (11) 12 - 7 = 5

Page **24** Halves

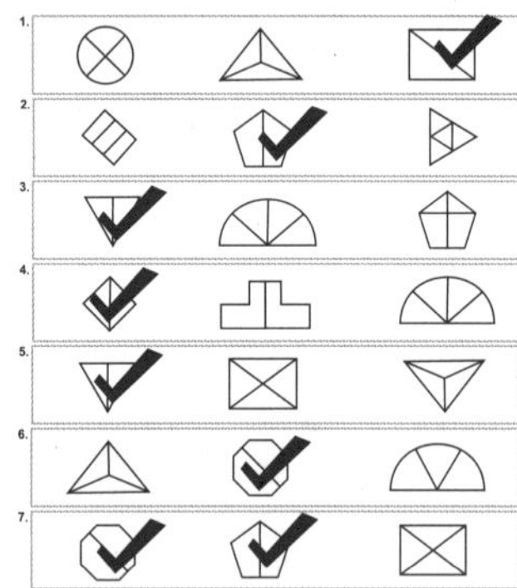

Page **25** Circle the Fractions

(1) $\frac{1}{3}$ (2) $\frac{1}{2}$ (3) $\frac{1}{4}$ (4) $\frac{1}{4}$ (5) $\frac{1}{2}$ (6) $\frac{1}{3}$ (7) $\frac{1}{2}$ (8) $\frac{1}{3}$ (9) $\frac{1}{4}$ (10) $\frac{1}{4}$ (11) $\frac{1}{3}$ (12) $\frac{1}{3}$

Page **27** Exploring Shapes

(1) Rectangle Number of Sides 4 Number of Angles 4
(2) Circle Number of Sides 0 Number of Angles 0
(3) Triangle Number of Sides 3 Number of Angles 3
(4) Square Number of Sides 4 Number of Angles 4
(5) Rhombus Number of Sides 4 Number of Angles
(6) Pentagon Number of Sides 5 Number of Angles

Answer Page

Here are some answer pages from math book grade one.

Page **30** Read and Follow the Directions

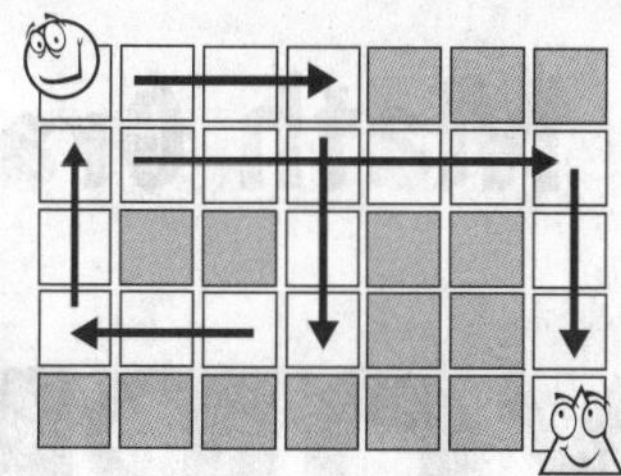

Page **31** Draw Shapes On The Grid

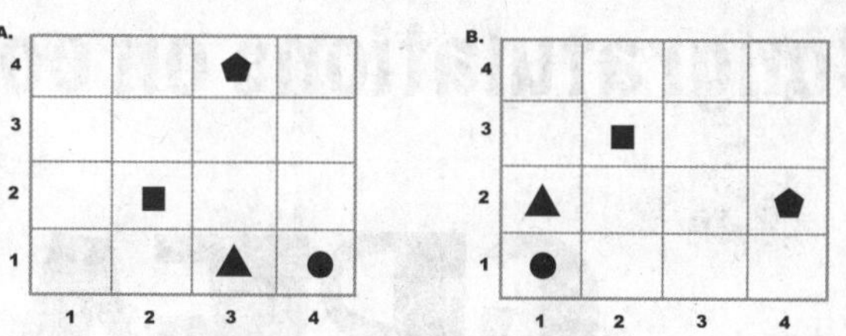

Page **32** Shapes Pictograph

(1) 4 (2) 2 (3) 3 (4) Circle (5) 9

?Page **33** Measurment: How Long?

(1) 9 (2) 6 (3) 3

Page **34** Tallest to Shortest

(1) 3, 1, 2 (2) 2, 3, 1

Page **35** Temperature: Hot and Cold

(1) Hot (2) Cold (3) Cold (4) Hot

Page **36** Extending Patterns

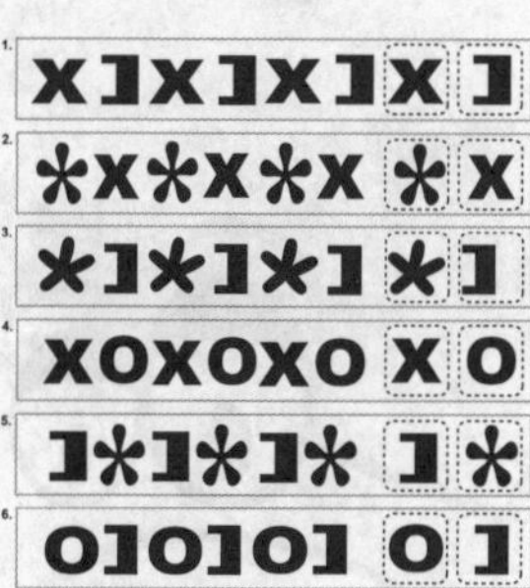

Page **37** Telling Time

Page **38** Telling Time to the Hour

(1) 12:00 (2) 7:00 (3) 1:00 (4) 3:00 (5) 6:00 (6) 11:00 (7) 5:00 (8) 2:00 (9) 10:00 (10) 8:00 (11) 4:00 (12) 9:00

Page **39** Telling Time to the Half Hour

(1) 11:30 (2) 3:30 (3) 7:30 (4) 12:30 (5) 4:30 (6) 9:30 (7) 10:30 (8) 5:30 (9) 8:30 (10) 1:30 (11) 6:30 (12) 2:30

Certificate of Completion

Congratulations on completing Math Grade 1

GREAT WORK!

Name: ______________________________